DREAM JOURNAL

Bella WordSmith

Dream Journal

Copyright © 2021 Epic WordSmiths

This Dream Journal belongs to

....

DREAM DATA

HUMAN BRAIN WAVES

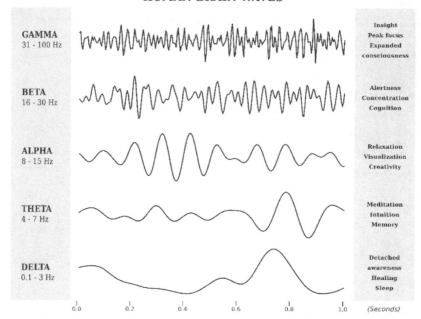

GAMMA 31 - 100 Hz		Insight Peak focus Expanded consciousness
BETA 16 - 30 Hz		Alertness Concentration Cognition
ALPHA 8 - 15 Hz		Relaxation Visualization Creativity
THETA 4 - 7 Hz		Meditation Intuition Memory
DELTA 0.1 - 3 Hz		Detached awareness Healing Sleep

0.0 0.2 0.4 0.6 0.8 1.0 *(Seconds)*

When we transition from our conscious brainwave states of Gamma and Beta down through our unconscious or sleeping states of Alpha, Theta and Delta our brainwaves gradually slow down. This is accompanied by consecutive periods of non-rapid eye movement (NREM) and rapid eye movement (REM) phases. It is mainly during the REM phases of sleep that we dream thus enabling us to attain both a deep state of rest and process information in the one 8-hour sleep cycle.

Dreams have various functions and benefits including:

- allowing our sub/unconscious minds to process aspects of our conscious minds that we might otherwise ignore, sometimes to our own detriment.
- reconnecting us with lost loved ones, soothing our souls & helping us recall & re-live cherished memories.

• DREAM DATA

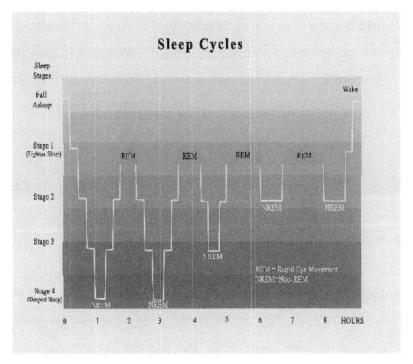

- analysing and sorting our short-term memory, storing important information in long-term memory and clearing irrelevant data - akin to deleting a computer's history cache whilst it's rebooting, freeing up memory space.
  - self-awareness, problem solving, creativity, fun, inspiration, fantasy, stress reduction, hormonal production and tissue restoration, physical and mental rest, reduction of depression and anxiety, wellbeing and ultimately survival.
- guiding our consciousness to become the spiritual people we were meant to be. Tibetan monks are said to experience lucid dreaming on their paths to spiritual enlightenment.

TYPES OF DREAMS

Standard: common dreams about everyday experiences and acquaintances including dreams about home, work & relationships.

Recurring: repeatedly dreaming of the same or similar themes/characters/locations/symbols/metaphors.

Archetypal: containing universal symbols such as the Hero, the Fool, the Empress, Justice, Death or the Moon.

Cultural: originating from within a group's beliefs and traditions i.e., Dreamtime for Australia's Indigenous People's.

Lucid: the dreamer is aware they are dreaming and may have some level of control over the outcome.

False Awakening: a vivid dream in which the dreamer believes they are awake but are actually still asleep – these types of dreams can result in sleep walking or other forms of parasomnia.

Precognitive: a dream that serves as a warning or is prophetic in some way, may include a call to action.

Incubative: the dreamer requests and receives specific information or an answer via their dreams.

Spiritual: an *epic* dream with ethereal qualities or symbols, may include spiritual guidance from a deity or messages from loved ones who have passed over, these highly memorable dreams enhance self-awareness, invoke strong emotions & an awe of the universe.

Nightmares/Terrors: Frighteningly realistic/distressing dreams which may lead to the dreamer acting out physically, sleep walking or sleep talking. Common nightmares include being chased, falling, dying, running late and encounters with snakes, lions or insects. May include sleep paralysis: an extreme form of night terror, where the dreamer is awake but cannot move and sometimes feels a weight upon them or the presence of someone or something foreboding.

TIPS FOR SWEET DREAMS

- Ensure you get adequate exercise & fresh air.
- Maintain a healthy diet including foods that contain the sleep enhancing amino-acid tryptophan such as cheese, chicken, and turkey, canned tuna, bananas, oats, nuts and seeds or a glass of luke-warm milk. Tryptophan plays a key role in the production of melatonin which regulates sleep patterns and serotonin that stabilizes mood.
- Avoid spicy foods, alcohol, cigarettes, non-prescribed drugs, horror movies (if you are prone to nightmares), and minimise the use of mobile phones & other electronic devices right before bedtime.
- Have a warm bath or shower before retiring and wear comfortable loose-fitting sleepwear. Ensure your bedding is comfortable with soft pillows & coverings that are not restrictive or too warm.
- Create an atmosphere conducive to sleep including a room that is quiet and well ventilated - the addition of some low-level white noise such as a fan, soft music or meditation soundtracks may assist if you find it difficult to get to doze off or if you wake during the night.
- Arrange an altar with natural elements such as herbs, oils, charms, crystals, stones, candles (in fire safe holders), a sage smudged dreamcatcher positioned over your bed.

- Form a sleeping ritual at the same time each evening including relaxation exercises and meditations and an affirmation to sleep peacefully & remember your dreams.
- Set your alarm 15 minutes early to give you time to recollect your dreams and to record and interpret them in your journal - consult a good dream dictionary for help with interpreting symbols, archetypes, and metaphors.
- It may be beneficial to seek professional support in analysing and resolving unwanted recurring dreams, nightmares, sleepwalking or other disturbing parasomnias.

Dream Catcher

Keep this journal by your bed,

a dream catcher above your head,

so as you sleep good dreams may come,

whilst legend says ,bad ones succumb

to spider webs spun through the night,

and disappear upon first light.

Bella WordSmith

Date

......./......./.........

Theme

....

Description

....
....
....
....
....
....
....
....
....
....
....
....
....
....
....
....
....
....
....
....

Characters & Archetypes

....

....

....

....

....

....

Symbols, Images & Metaphors & Locations

....

....

....

....

....

....

Interpretation & Notes

....

....

....

....

....

....

....

....

Dream Type
Standard
Recurring
Archetypal
Cultural
Lucid
False Awake
Precognitive
Incubative
Spiritual
Nightmare

Dream Emoji

Date

....../......./.........

Theme

....

Description

....
....
....
....
....
....
....
....
....
....
....
....
....
....
....
....
....
....

Characters & Archetypes

....

....

....

....

....

....

Symbols, Images & Metaphors & Locations

....

....

....

....

....

Interpretation & Notes

....

....

....

....

....

....

....

....

Dream Type
Standard
Recurring
Archetypal
Cultural
Lucid
False Awake
Precognitive
Incubative
Spiritual
Nightmare

Dream Emoji

Date

......../......../..........

Theme

....

Description

....
....
....
....
....
....
....
....
....
....
....
....
....
....
....
....
....

Characters & Archetypes

....

....

....

....

....

....

Symbols, Images & Metaphors & Locations

....

....

....

....

....

....

Interpretation & Notes

....

....

....

....

....

....

....

....

Dream Type
Standard
Recurring
Archetypal
Cultural
Lucid
False Awake
Precognitive
Incubative
Spiritual
Nightmare

Dream Emoji

Date

....../......../.........

Theme

....

Description

....
....
....
....
....
....
....
....
....
....
....
....
....
....
....
....
....
....

Characters & Archetypes

....

....

....

....

....

....

Symbols, Images & Metaphors & Locations

....

....

....

....

....

....

Interpretation & Notes

....

....

....

....

....

....

....

....

Dream Type
Standard
Recurring
Archetypal
Cultural
Lucid
False Awake
Precognitive
Incubative
Spiritual
Nightmare

Dream Emoji

Date

....../........./.........

Theme

....

Description

....
....
....
....
....
....
....
....
....
....
....
....
....
....
....
....
....
....

Characters & Archetypes

....

....

....

....

....

....

Symbols, Images & Metaphors & Locations

....

....

....

....

....

Interpretation & Notes

....

....

....

....

....

....

....

Dream Type
Standard
Recurring
Archetypal
Cultural
Lucid
False Awake
Precognitive
Incubative
Spiritual
Nightmare

Dream Emoji

Date

....../......../.........

Theme

···

Description

···
···
···
···
···
···
···
···
···
···
···
···
···
···
···
···
···
···

Characters & Archetypes

....

....

....

....

....

....

Symbols, Images & Metaphors & Locations

....

....

....

....

....

....

Interpretation & Notes

....

....

....

....

....

....

....

....

Dream Type
Standard
Recurring
Archetypal
Cultural
Lucid
False Awake
Precognitive
Incubative
Spiritual
Nightmare

Dream Emoji

Date

....../......./.........

Theme

....

Description

....
....
....
....
....
....
....
....
....
....
....
....
....
....
....
....
....
....
....

Characters & Archetypes

....

....

....

....

....

....

Symbols, Images & Metaphors & Locations

....

....

....

....

....

....

Interpretation & Notes

....

....

....

....

....

....

....

....

Dream Type
Standard
Recurring
Archetypal
Cultural
Lucid
False Awake
Precognitive
Incubative
Spiritual
Nightmare
Dream Emoji

Date

....../......../.........

Theme

··

Description

··
··
··
··
··
··
··
··
··
··
··
··
··
··
··
··
··
··

Characters & Archetypes

. . . .

. . . .

. . . .

. . . .

. . . .

. . . .

Symbols, Images & Metaphors & Locations

. . . .

. . . .

. . . .

. . . .

. . . .

Interpretation & Notes

. . . .

. . . .

. . . .

. . . .

. . . .

. . . .

. . . .

. . . .

Dream Type
Standard
Recurring
Archetypal
Cultural
Lucid
False Awake
Precognitive
Incubative
Spiritual
Nightmare

Dream Emoji
🙂
🙁
😐
😳
😮
😎
🤡
🤬
😇
💀

Date

....../......../.........

Theme

....

Description

....
....
....
....
....
....
....
....
....
....
....
....
....
....
....
....
....
....

Characters & Archetypes

· ·

· ·

· ·

· ·

· ·

· ·

Symbols, Images & Metaphors & Locations

· ·

· ·

· ·

· ·

· ·

· ·

Interpretation & Notes

· ·

· ·

· ·

· ·

· ·

· ·

· ·

Dream Type
Standard
Recurring
Archetypal
Cultural
Lucid
False Awake
Precognitive
Incubative
Spiritual
Nightmare

Dream Emoji

Date

....../......../.........

Theme

....

Description

....
....
....
....
....
....
....
....
....
....
....
....
....
....
....
....
....
....

Characters & Archetypes

....
....
....
....
....
....

Symbols, Images & Metaphors & Locations

....
....
....
....
....
....

Interpretation & Notes

....
....
....
....
....
....
....
....

Dream Type
Standard
Recurring
Archetypal
Cultural
Lucid
False Awake
Precognitive
Incubative
Spiritual
Nightmare

Dream Emoji

Date

....../......../.........

Theme

....

Description

....
....
....
....
....
....
....
....
....
....
....
....
....
....
....
....
....
....

Characters & Archetypes

....

....

....

....

....

....

Symbols, Images & Metaphors & Locations

....

....

....

....

....

Interpretation & Notes

....

....

....

....

....

....

....

....

Dream Type
Standard
Recurring
Archetypal
Cultural
Lucid
False Awake
Precognitive
Incubative
Spiritual
Nightmare

Dream Emoji

Date

....../......../........

Theme

....

Description

....
....
....
....
....
....
....
....
....
....
....
....
....
....
....
....
....

Characters & Archetypes

....

....

....

....

....

....

Symbols, Images & Metaphors & Locations

....

....

....

....

....

....

Interpretation & Notes

....

....

....

....

....

....

....

Dream Type
Standard
Recurring
Archetypal
Cultural
Lucid
False Awake
Precognitive
Incubative
Spiritual
Nightmare

Dream Emoji

Date

....../......../.........

Theme

....

Description

....
....
....
....
....
....
....
....
....
....
....
....
....
....
....
....
....
....

Characters & Archetypes

....

....

....

....

....

....

Symbols, Images & Metaphors & Locations

....

....

....

....

....

....

Interpretation & Notes

....

....

....

....

....

....

....

....

Dream Type
Standard
Recurring
Archetypal
Cultural
Lucid
False Awake
Precognitive
Incubative
Spiritual
Nightmare

Dream Emoji

Date

......./......../.........

Theme

··

Description

··

··

··

··

··

··

··

··

··

··

··

··

··

··

··

··

··

··

··

Characters & Archetypes

....
....
....
....
....
....

Symbols, Images & Metaphors & Locations

....
....
....
....
....
....

Interpretation & Notes

....
....
....
....
....
....
....
....

Dream Type
Standard
Recurring
Archetypal
Cultural
Lucid
False Awake
Precognitive
Incubative
Spiritual
Nightmare

Dream Emoji

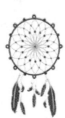

Date

....../......../.........

Theme

....

Description

....
....
....
....
....
....
....
....
....
....
....
....
....
....
....
....
....

Characters & Archetypes

....

....

....

....

....

....

Symbols, Images & Metaphors & Locations

....

....

....

....

....

....

Interpretation & Notes

....

....

....

....

....

....

....

Dream Type
Standard
Recurring
Archetypal
Cultural
Lucid
False Awake
Precognitive
Incubative
Spiritual
Nightmare

Dream Emoji
😀
😟
😐
😕
😨
😎
🤡
🤬
😇
💀

Date

....../......../.........

Theme

....

Description

....
....
....
....
....
....
....
....
....
....
....
....
....
....
....
....
....
....

Characters & Archetypes

....

....

....

....

....

....

Symbols, Images & Metaphors & Locations

....

....

....

....

....

Interpretation & Notes

....

....

....

....

....

....

....

....

....

Dream Type
Standard
Recurring
Archetypal
Cultural
Lucid
False Awake
Precognitive
Incubative
Spiritual
Nightmare

Dream Emoji
😃
🙁
😐
🙄
😦
😍
🤡
🤬
😇
💀

Date

....../ ..../ ....

Theme

....

Description

....
....
....
....
....
....
....
....
....
....
....
....
....
....
....
....
....
....

Characters & Archetypes

. . . .

. . . .

. . . .

. . . .

. . . .

. . . .

Symbols, Images & Metaphors & Locations

. . . .

. . . .

. . . .

. . . .

. . . .

Interpretation & Notes

. . . .

. . . .

. . . .

. . . .

. . . .

. . . .

. . . .

Dream Type
Standard
Recurring
Archetypal
Cultural
Lucid
False Awake
Precognitive
Incubative
Spiritual
Nightmare

Dream Emoji

Date

....../......../.........

Theme

....

Description

....
....
....
....
....
....
....
....
....
....
....
....
....
....
....
....
....
....

Characters & Archetypes

· ·

· ·

· ·

· ·

· ·

· ·

Symbols, Images & Metaphors & Locations

· ·

· ·

· ·

· ·

· ·

· ·

Interpretation & Notes

· ·

· ·

· ·

· ·

· ·

· ·

· ·

Dream Type
Standard
Recurring
Archetypal
Cultural
Lucid
False Awake
Precognitive
Incubative
Spiritual
Nightmare

Dream Emoji
😀
🙁
😐
🙄
😦
😎
🤡
🤬
😇
💀

Date

....../......../.........

Theme

· ·

Description

· ·
· ·
· ·
· ·
· ·
· ·
· ·
· ·
· ·
· ·
· ·
· ·
· ·
· ·
· ·
· ·
· ·

Characters & Archetypes

....

....

....

....

....

....

Symbols, Images & Metaphors & Locations

....

....

....

....

....

Interpretation & Notes

....

....

....

....

....

....

....

Dream Type
Standard
Recurring
Archetypal
Cultural
Lucid
False Awake
Precognitive
Incubative
Spiritual
Nightmare
Dream Emoji

Date

....../......../.........

Theme

....

Description

....
....
....
....
....
....
....
....
....
....
....
....
....
....
....
....
....
....
....

Characters & Archetypes

....

....

....

....

....

....

Symbols, Images & Metaphors & Locations

....

....

....

....

....

....

....

Interpretation & Notes

....

....

....

....

....

....

....

....

Dream Type
Standard
Recurring
Archetypal
Cultural
Lucid
False Awake
Precognitive
Incubative
Spiritual
Nightmare

Dream Emoji

Date

......./........./.........

Theme

....

Description

....

....

....

....

....

....

....

....

....

....

....

....

....

....

....

....

....

Characters & Archetypes

....

....

....

....

....

....

Symbols, Images & Metaphors & Locations

....

....

....

....

....

....

Interpretation & Notes

....

....

....

....

....

....

....

Dream Type
Standard
Recurring
Archetypal
Cultural
Lucid
False Awake
Precognitive
Incubative
Spiritual
Nightmare
Dream Emoji

Date

....../ ..../ ....

Theme

....

Description

....
....
....
....
....
....
....
....
....
....
....
....
....
....
....
....
....
....

Characters & Archetypes

....
....
....
....
....
....

Symbols, Images & Metaphors & Locations

....
....
....
....
....
....

Interpretation & Notes

....
....
....
....
....
....
....
....

Dream Type
Standard
Recurring
Archetypal
Cultural
Lucid
False Awake
Precognitive
Incubative
Spiritual
Nightmare
Dream Emoji

Date

....../......../.........

Theme

....

Description

....
....
....
....
....
....
....
....
....
....
....
....
....
....
....
....
....
....

Characters & Archetypes

....

....

....

....

....

....

Symbols, Images & Metaphors & Locations

....

....

....

....

....

Interpretation & Notes

....

....

....

....

....

....

....

Dream Type
Standard
Recurring
Archetypal
Cultural
Lucid
False Awake
Precognitive
Incubative
Spiritual
Nightmare

Dream Emoji
😃
🙁
😐
😦
😮
😎
🤡
🤬
😇
💀

Date

......./......../.........

Theme

···

Description

···
···
···
···
···
···
···
···
···
···
···
···
···
···
···
···
···

Characters & Archetypes

....
....
....
....
....
....

Symbols, Images & Metaphors & Locations

....
....
....
....
....
....

Interpretation & Notes

....
....
....
....
....
....
....
....

Dream Type
Standard
Recurring
Archetypal
Cultural
Lucid
False Awake
Precognitive
Incubative
Spiritual
Nightmare
Dream Emoji

Date

....../......../.........

Theme

....

Description

....
....
....
....
....
....
....
....
....
....
....
....
....
....
....
....
....
....
....
....

Characters & Archetypes

....
....
....
....
....
....

Symbols, Images & Metaphors & Locations

....
....
....
....
....
....

Interpretation & Notes

....
....
....
....
....
....
....
....

Dream Type
Standard
Recurring
Archetypal
Cultural
Lucid
False Awake
Precognitive
Incubative
Spiritual
Nightmare
Dream Emoji

Date

....../......./.........

Theme

....

Description

....
....
....
....
....
....
....
....
....
....
....
....
....
....
....
....
....
....

Characters & Archetypes

....

....

....

....

....

....

Symbols, Images & Metaphors & Locations

....

....

....

....

....

Interpretation & Notes

....

....

....

....

....

....

....

....

Dream Type
Standard
Recurring
Archetypal
Cultural
Lucid
False Awake
Precognitive
Incubative
Spiritual
Nightmare
Dream Emoji

Date

......../........../.........

Theme

....

Description

....

....

....

....

....

....

....

....

....

....

....

....

....

....

....

....

....

Characters & Archetypes

....
....
....
....
....
....

Symbols, Images & Metaphors & Locations

....
....
....
....
....
....

Interpretation & Notes

....
....
....
....
....
....
....

Dream Type
Standard
Recurring
Archetypal
Cultural
Lucid
False Awake
Precognitive
Incubative
Spiritual
Nightmare
Dream Emoji

Date

....../......./.........

Theme

....

Description

....
....
....
....
....
....
....
....
....
....
....
....
....
....
....
....
....
....

Characters & Archetypes

....

....

....

....

....

....

Symbols, Images & Metaphors & Locations

....

....

....

....

....

....

Interpretation & Notes

....

....

....

....

....

....

....

....

Dream Type
Standard
Recurring
Archetypal
Cultural
Lucid
False Awake
Precognitive
Incubative
Spiritual
Nightmare

Dream Emoji

Date

...... / .... / ....

Theme

....

Description

....
....
....
....
....
....
....
....
....
....
....
....
....
....
....
....
....
....

Characters & Archetypes

....

....

....

....

....

....

Symbols, Images & Metaphors & Locations

....

....

....

....

....

....

Interpretation & Notes

....

....

....

....

....

....

....

Dream Type
Standard
Recurring
Archetypal
Cultural
Lucid
False Awake
Precognitive
Incubative
Spiritual
Nightmare
Dream Emoji

Date

....../......../........

Theme

....

Description

....
....
....
....
....
....
....
....
....
....
....
....
....
....
....
....
....
....

Characters & Archetypes

. . . .

. . . .

. . . .

. . . .

. . . .

. . . .

Symbols, Images & Metaphors & Locations

. . . .

. . . .

. . . .

. . . .

. . . .

. . . .

Interpretation & Notes

. . . .

. . . .

. . . .

. . . .

. . . .

. . . .

. . . .

Dream Type
Standard
Recurring
Archetypal
Cultural
Lucid
False Awake
Precognitive
Incubative
Spiritual
Nightmare

Dream Emoji

Date

....../......../.........

Theme

....

Description

....
....
....
....
....
....
....
....
....
....
....
....
....
....
....
....
....

Characters & Archetypes

....

....

....

....

....

....

Symbols, Images & Metaphors & Locations

....

....

....

....

....

....

Interpretation & Notes

....

....

....

....

....

....

....

....

Dream Type
Standard
Recurring
Archetypal
Cultural
Lucid
False Awake
Precognitive
Incubative
Spiritual
Nightmare
Dream Emoji

Date

....../......./........

Theme

....

Description

....
....
....
....
....
....
....
....
....
....
....
....
....
....
....
....
....

Characters & Archetypes

....

....

....

....

....

....

Symbols, Images & Metaphors & Locations

....

....

....

....

....

....

Interpretation & Notes

....

....

....

....

....

....

....

....

Dream Type
Standard
Recurring
Archetypal
Cultural
Lucid
False Awake
Precognitive
Incubative
Spiritual
Nightmare

Dream Emoji

Date

....../......../.........

Theme

....

Description

....
....
....
....
....
....
....
....
....
....
....
....
....
....
....
....
....

Characters & Archetypes

....

....

....

....

....

....

Symbols, Images & Metaphors & Locations

....

....

....

....

....

Interpretation & Notes

....

....

....

....

....

....

....

Dream Type
Standard
Recurring
Archetypal
Cultural
Lucid
False Awake
Precognitive
Incubative
Spiritual
Nightmare

Dream Emoji

Date

......./......../.........

Theme

....

Description

....
....
....
....
....
....
....
....
....
....
....
....
....
....
....
....
....

Characters & Archetypes

....

....

....

....

....

....

Symbols, Images & Metaphors & Locations

....

....

....

....

....

....

Interpretation & Notes

....

....

....

....

....

....

....

....

Dream Type
Standard
Recurring
Archetypal
Cultural
Lucid
False Awake
Precognitive
Incubative
Spiritual
Nightmare

Dream Emoji
😀
🙁
😐
🙄
😮
😎
🤡
🤬
😇
💀

Date

....../........./.........

Theme

....

Description

....
....
....
....
....
....
....
....
....
....
....
....
....
....
....
....
....
....

Characters & Archetypes

....

....

....

....

....

....

Symbols, Images & Metaphors & Locations

....

....

....

....

....

....

Interpretation & Notes

....

....

....

....

....

....

....

....

Dream Type
Standard
Recurring
Archetypal
Cultural
Lucid
False Awake
Precognitive
Incubative
Spiritual
Nightmare

Dream Emoji

Date

....../......../.........

Theme

....

Description

....
....
....
....
....
....
....
....
....
....
....
....
....
....
....
....

Characters & Archetypes

....
....
....
....
....
....

Symbols, Images & Metaphors & Locations

....
....
....
....
....
....

Interpretation & Notes

....
....
....
....
....
....
....
....

Dream Type
Standard
Recurring
Archetypal
Cultural
Lucid
False Awake
Precognitive
Incubative
Spiritual
Nightmare
Dream Emoji

Date

....../......./.........

Theme

....

Description

....
....
....
....
....
....
....
....
....
....
....
....
....
....
....
....
....
....

Characters & Archetypes

....
....
....
....
....
....

Symbols, Images & Metaphors & Locations

....
....
....
....
....
....

Interpretation & Notes

....
....
....
....
....
....
....
....

Dream Type
Standard
Recurring
Archetypal
Cultural
Lucid
False Awake
Precognitive
Incubative
Spiritual
Nightmare

Dream Emoji

Date

....../......../.........

Theme

··

Description

··
··
··
··
··
··
··
··
··
··
··
··
··
··
··
··
··

Characters & Archetypes

....
....
....
....
....
....

Symbols, Images & Metaphors & Locations

....
....
....
....
....

Interpretation & Notes

....
....
....
....
....
....
....

Dream Type
Standard
Recurring
Archetypal
Cultural
Lucid
False Awake
Precognitive
Incubative
Spiritual
Nightmare
Dream Emoji

Date

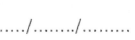

......./........../.........

Theme

....

Description

....
....
....
....
....
....
....
....
....
....
....
....
....
....
....
....
....

Characters & Archetypes

....

....

....

....

....

....

Symbols, Images & Metaphors & Locations

....

....

....

....

....

Interpretation & Notes

....

....

....

....

....

....

....

Dream Type
Standard
Recurring
Archetypal
Cultural
Lucid
False Awake
Precognitive
Incubative
Spiritual
Nightmare

Dream Emoji

Date

......./......../.........

Theme

....

Description

....
....
....
....
....
....
....
....
....
....
....
....
....
....
....
....
....
....
....

Characters & Archetypes

....

....

....

....

....

....

....

Symbols, Images & Metaphors & Locations

....

....

....

....

....

....

Interpretation & Notes

....

....

....

....

....

....

....

....

Dream Type
Standard
Recurring
Archetypal
Cultural
Lucid
False Awake
Precognitive
Incubative
Spiritual
Nightmare

Dream Emoji

Date

....../......../.........

Theme

....

Description

....
....
....
....
....
....
....
....
....
....
....
....
....
....
....
....
....
....
....

Characters & Archetypes

....

....

....

....

....

....

Symbols, Images & Metaphors & Locations

....

....

....

....

....

....

Interpretation & Notes

....

....

....

....

....

....

....

....

Dream Type
Standard
Recurring
Archetypal
Cultural
Lucid
False Awake
Precognitive
Incubative
Spiritual
Nightmare

Dream Emoji

Date

....../........../.........

Theme

···

Description

···
···
···
···
···
···
···
···
···
···
···
···
···
···
···
···
···
···

Characters & Archetypes

....

....

....

....

....

....

Symbols, Images & Metaphors & Locations

....

....

....

....

....

Interpretation & Notes

....

....

....

....

....

....

....

Dream Type
Standard
Recurring
Archetypal
Cultural
Lucid
False Awake
Precognitive
Incubative
Spiritual
Nightmare
Dream Emoji

Date

...../......./.........

Theme

....

Description

....
....
....
....
....
....
....
....
....
....
....
....
....
....
....
....
....

Characters & Archetypes

....

....

....

....

....

....

Symbols, Images & Metaphors & Locations

....

....

....

....

....

....

Interpretation & Notes

....

....

....

....

....

....

....

....

Dream Type
Standard
Recurring
Archetypal
Cultural
Lucid
False Awake
Precognitive
Incubative
Spiritual
Nightmare
Dream Emoji

Date

......./......../.........

Theme

....

Description

....
....
....
....
....
....
....
....
....
....
....
....
....
....
....
....
....
....
....

Characters & Archetypes

....

....

....

....

....

....

....

Symbols, Images & Metaphors & Locations

....

....

....

....

....

....

Interpretation & Notes

....

....

....

....

....

....

....

....

Dream Type
Standard
Recurring
Archetypal
Cultural
Lucid
False Awake
Precognitive
Incubative
Spiritual
Nightmare

Dream Emoji
😀
😟
😐
😨
😮
😍
🤡
🤬
😇
💀

Date

....../......./.........

Theme

....

Description

....
....
....
....
....
....
....
....
....
....
....
....
....
....
....
....
....

Characters & Archetypes

....

....

....

....

....

....

Symbols, Images & Metaphors & Locations

....

....

....

....

....

Interpretation & Notes

....

....

....

....

....

....

....

Dream Type
Standard
Recurring
Archetypal
Cultural
Lucid
False Awake
Precognitive
Incubative
Spiritual
Nightmare

Dream Emoji
😃
🙁
😐
😦
😮
😍
🤡
🤬
😇
💀

Date

....../......./.........

Theme

....

Description

....
....
....
....
....
....
....
....
....
....
....
....
....
....
....
....
....
....

Characters & Archetypes

....

....

....

....

....

....

Symbols, Images & Metaphors & Locations

....

....

....

....

....

....

Interpretation & Notes

....

....

....

....

....

....

....

....

Dream Type
Standard
Recurring
Archetypal
Cultural
Lucid
False Awake
Precognitive
Incubative
Spiritual
Nightmare

Dream Emoji
😃
🙁
😐
🙄
😮
😎
🤡
🤬
😇
💀

Date

....../......../.........

Theme

....

Description

....
....
....
....
....
....
....
....
....
....
....
....
....
....
....
....
....
....

Characters & Archetypes

....
....
....
....
....
....

Symbols, Images & Metaphors & Locations

....
....
....
....
....

Interpretation & Notes

....
....
....
....
....
....
....

Dream Type
Standard
Recurring
Archetypal
Cultural
Lucid
False Awake
Precognitive
Incubative
Spiritual
Nightmare

Dream Emoji

Date

....../........./.........

Theme

....

Description

....
....
....
....
....
....
....
....
....
....
....
....
....
....
....
....
....

Characters & Archetypes

....

....

....

....

....

....

Symbols, Images & Metaphors & Locations

....

....

....

....

....

....

Interpretation & Notes

....

....

....

....

....

....

....

Dream Type
Standard
Recurring
Archetypal
Cultural
Lucid
False Awake
Precognitive
Incubative
Spiritual
Nightmare

Dream Emoji

Date

....../......../.........

Theme

···

Description

···
···
···
···
···
···
···
···
···
···
···
···
···
···
···
···
···
···
···

Characters & Archetypes

....

....

....

....

....

....

Symbols, Images & Metaphors & Locations

....

....

....

....

....

Interpretation & Notes

....

....

....

....

....

....

....

....

Dream Type
Standard
Recurring
Archetypal
Cultural
Lucid
False Awake
Precognitive
Incubative
Spiritual
Nightmare
Dream Emoji

Date

...... / .... / ....

Theme

....

Description

....
....
....
....
....
....
....
....
....
....
....
....
....
....
....
....
....
....

Characters & Archetypes

....

....

....

....

....

....

Symbols, Images & Metaphors & Locations

....

....

....

....

....

....

Interpretation & Notes

....

....

....

....

....

....

....

....

Dream Type
Standard
Recurring
Archetypal
Cultural
Lucid
False Awake
Precognitive
Incubative
Spiritual
Nightmare

Dream Emoji

Date

...... / .... / ....

Theme

··

Description

··
··
··
··
··
··
··
··
··
··
··
··
··
··
··
··
··

Characters & Archetypes

....

....

....

....

....

....

Symbols, Images & Metaphors & Locations

....

....

....

....

....

Interpretation & Notes

....

....

....

....

....

....

....

....

Dream Type
Standard
Recurring
Archetypal
Cultural
Lucid
False Awake
Precognitive
Incubative
Spiritual
Nightmare

Dream Emoji

Date

......./......../.........

Theme

....

Description

....
....
....
....
....
....
....
....
....
....
....
....
....
....
....
....
....
....

Characters & Archetypes

....

....

....

....

....

....

Symbols, Images & Metaphors & Locations

....

....

....

....

....

....

Interpretation & Notes

....

....

....

....

....

....

....

....

Dream Type
Standard
Recurring
Archetypal
Cultural
Lucid
False Awake
Precognitive
Incubative
Spiritual
Nightmare

Dream Emoji

Date

......./......../.........

Theme

....

Description

....
....
....
....
....
....
....
....
....
....
....
....
....
....
....
....
....
....

Characters & Archetypes

....
....
....
....
....
....

Symbols, Images & Metaphors & Locations

....
....
....
....
....

Interpretation & Notes

....
....
....
....
....
....
....
....

Dream Type
Standard
Recurring
Archetypal
Cultural
Lucid
False Awake
Precognitive
Incubative
Spiritual
Nightmare
Dream Emoji

Date

....../......../.........

Theme

....

Description

....

....

....

....

....

....

....

....

....

....

....

....

....

....

....

....

....

Characters & Archetypes

....

....

....

....

....

....

Symbols, Images & Metaphors & Locations

....

....

....

....

....

Interpretation & Notes

....

....

....

....

....

....

....

....

Dream Type
Standard
Recurring
Archetypal
Cultural
Lucid
False Awake
Precognitive
Incubative
Spiritual
Nightmare

Dream Emoji

Date

Theme

....

Description

....
....
....
....
....
....
....
....
....
....
....
....
....
....
....
....
....
....

Characters & Archetypes

....

....

....

....

....

....

Symbols, Images & Metaphors & Locations

....

....

....

....

....

....

Interpretation & Notes

....

....

....

....

....

....

....

....

Dream Type
Standard
Recurring
Archetypal
Cultural
Lucid
False Awake
Precognitive
Incubative
Spiritual
Nightmare
Dream Emoji

Date

....../......../.........

Theme

....

Description

....
....
....
....
....
....
....
....
....
....
....
....
....
....
....
....
....
....

Characters & Archetypes

....
....
....
....
....
....

Symbols, Images & Metaphors & Locations

....
....
....
....
....

Interpretation & Notes

....
....
....
....
....
....
....
....

Dream Type
Standard
Recurring
Archetypal
Cultural
Lucid
False Awake
Precognitive
Incubative
Spiritual
Nightmare
Dream Emoji

Date

....../......../.........

Theme

....

Description

....
....
....
....
....
....
....
....
....
....
....
....
....
....
....
....
....

Characters & Archetypes

....
....
....
....
....
....

Symbols, Images & Metaphors & Locations

....
....
....
....
....

Interpretation & Notes

....
....
....
....
....
....
....
....

Dream Type
Standard
Recurring
Archetypal
Cultural
Lucid
False Awake
Precognitive
Incubative
Spiritual
Nightmare

Dream Emoji

Date

......./......../.........

Theme

....

Description

....
....
....
....
....
....
....
....
....
....
....
....
....
....
....
....
....

Characters & Archetypes

....

....

....

....

....

....

Symbols, Images & Metaphors & Locations

....

....

....

....

....

Interpretation & Notes

....

....

....

....

....

....

....

Dream Type
Standard
Recurring
Archetypal
Cultural
Lucid
False Awake
Precognitive
Incubative
Spiritual
Nightmare
Dream Emoji

Dream Journal Summary

Dream Type	Total	Dream Emoji	Total
Standard		😃	
Recurring		😢	
Archetypal		😐	
Cultural		🙄	
Lucid		😮	
False Awake		😍	
Precognitive		🤡	
Incubative		🤬	
Spiritual		😇	
Nightmare		💀	

Dream Journal Review

What are my top 3 dream types?

....

....

....

What are my top 3 dream emojis?

What insights can I gain from these results?

....
....
....
....
....
....
....
....
....
....
....
....

Notes

Notes

....
....
....
....
....
....
....
....
....
....
....
....
....
....
....
....
....
....
....
....
....
....
....
....
....
....
....

With many thanks to:

my Sons, my Mum, my Sister, my Best Friend and her Mum
for listening to my crazy, cryptic and convoluted dreams and
for helping me to make sense of them, believe in them and in myself

Credits

Cover Image: Pixabay, Ractapopulous, 1981152

Sleeping Owl Image: VectorStock.com, Microstocksec, 4564693

Moon Image: Pixabay, Pixel2013, 3069469

Dreamcatcher Image: Pixabay, Kirsten Star, 1788485

Brainwave Image: Shutterstock, Artellia, 249216236

Sleep Cycle Image: Shutterstock, Arka38, 1198377799

Sweet Dreams Image: Shutterstock, Elena Emchuk, 1853785126

Dreamcatcher Image: Shutterstock, Galunga.art, 1689058930

Moon and Stars Image: Shutterstock, Bepoh624, 1731206635

Milky Way Image: Pixabay, Moos Media, 2338185

Jung, C. (1934). The Meaning of Psychology for Modern Man.
Retrieved from https://en.wikiquote.org/wiki/Carl_Jung

Freud, S. (1900). The Interpretation of Dreams. Retrieved from
https://goodreads.com/work/quotes/1758256-die-traumdeutung

We hope that you are happy with your purchase of this

Dream Journal

and that it has made your dreams more enjoyable and insightful.

If by any chance the book you have received is damaged or defective,

you may return it to Amazon for a replacement or refund
within 30 days of purchase.

We would really appreciate it if you left an honest review

on Amazon at your earliest convenience using your country's link at:

http://www.amazon.com/review/create-review?&asin=B08XS7CD5P

http://www.amazon.co.uk/review/create-review?&asin=B08XS7CD5P

http://www.amazon.com.au/review/create-review?&asin=B08XS7CD5P

http://www.amazon.ca/review/create-review?&asin=B08XS7CD5P

or by scanning your country's QR code:

US	UK	AUS	CAN

You can also check out our other books at:

amazon.com/author/epic-wordsmiths_4_an_epic_life

Made in the USA
Las Vegas, NV
08 November 2024

11370761R00075